1 Piano, 4 Hands / Intermediate

ADELE FOR PIANO DUET

Arranged by Eric Baumgartner

Cover photo: Sascha Steinbach / Stringer Getty Images Entertainment

ISBN 978-1-4950-6906-2

HAL•LEONARD®
CORPORATION
7777 W. BLUEMOUND RD. P.O. BOX 13819 MILWAUKEE, WI 53213

Visit Hal Leonard Online at
www.halleonard.com

CHASING PAVEMENTS

Should I give up, or should I just keep chasing pavements even if it leads nowhere?
Or would it be a waste even if I knew my place? Should I leave it there?

Words and Music by ADELE ADKINS
and FRANCIS EG WHITE

6

CODA

HELLO

Hello, can you hear me?
I'm in California, dreaming about who we used to be when we were younger and free.
I've forgotten how it felt before the world fell at our feet.

Words and Music by ADELE ADKINS
and GREG KURSTIN

MAKE YOU FEEL MY LOVE

When the evening shadows and the stars appear, and there is no one there to dry your tears,
I could hold you for a million years to make you feel my love.

Words and Music by
BOB DYLAN

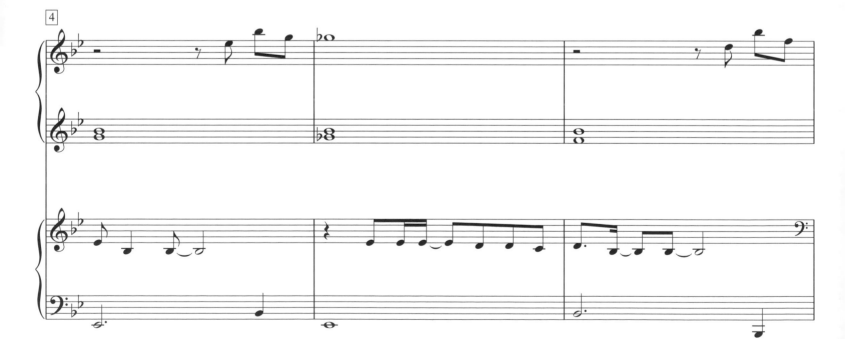

14

ROLLING IN THE DEEP

The scars of your love remind me of us, they keep me thinking that we almost had it all.
The scars of your love, they leave me breathless, I can't help feeling we could have had it all.

Words and Music by ADELE ADKINS
and PAUL EPWORTH

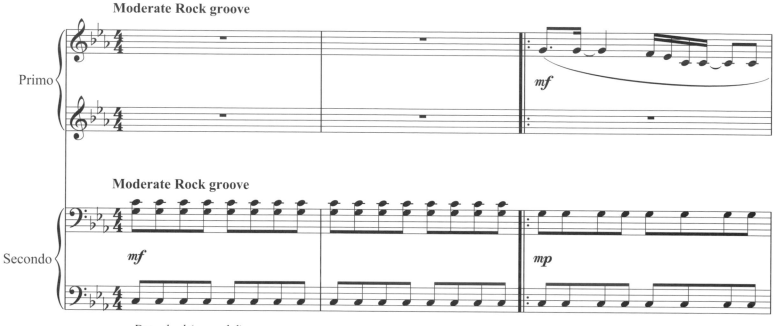

SET FIRE TO THE RAIN

But there's a side to you that I never knew. All the things you'd say, they were never true.
And the games you'd play, you would always win.
But I set fire to the rain, watched it pour as I touched your face.
When it burned, I cried, 'cause I heard it screaming out your name.

Words and Music by ADELE ADKINS
and FRASER SMITH

With light pedal

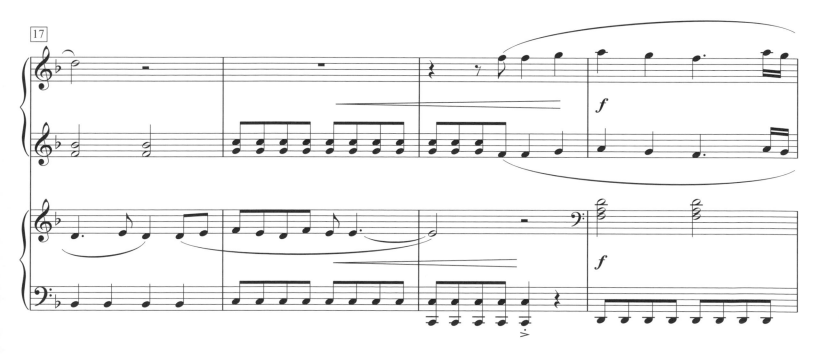

SKYFALL
from the Motion Picture SKYFALL

Let the sky fall: when it crumbles, we will stand tall, face it all together at Skyfall.

Words and Music by ADELE ADKINS
and PAUL EPWORTH

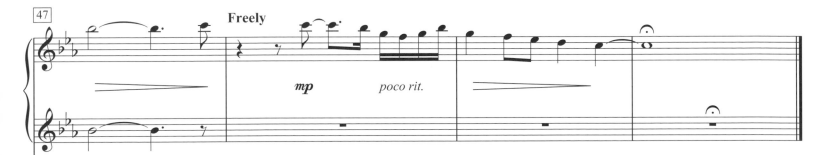

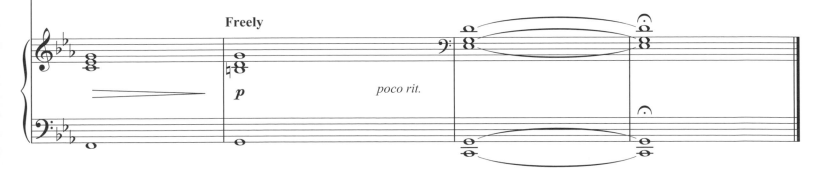

SOMEONE LIKE YOU

You know how the time flies, only yesterday was the time of our lives.
We were born in a summer haze, bound by the surprise of our glory days.
I hate to turn up out of the blue uninvited, but I couldn't stay away, I couldn't fight it.
I had hoped you'd see my face and that you'd be reminded that, for me, it isn't over.

Words and Music by ADELE ADKINS
and DAN WILSON

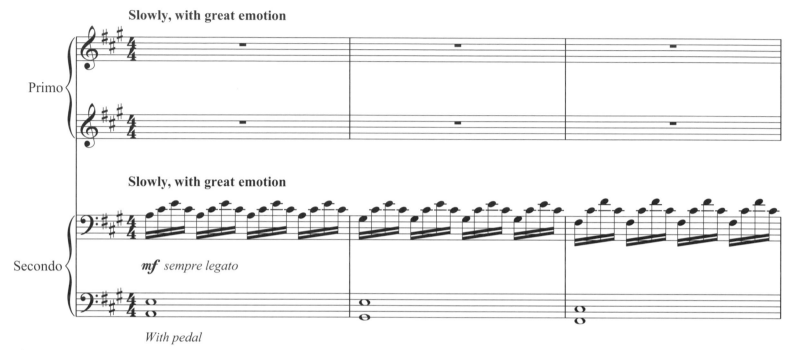

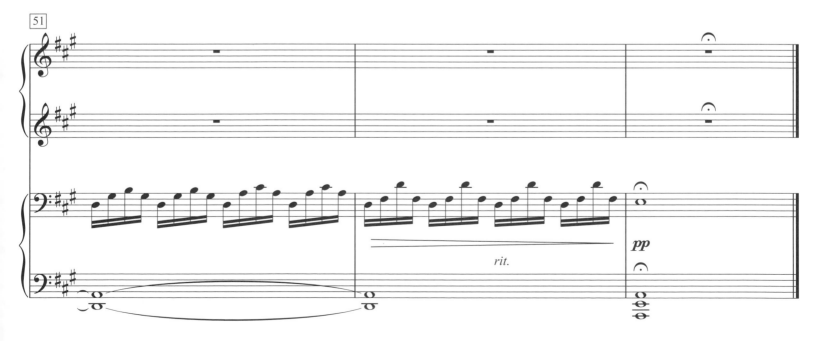

WHEN WE WERE YOUNG

Let me photograph you in this light, in case it is the last time that we might
Be exactly like we were before we realized we were sad of getting old, it made us restless;
It was just like a movie, it was just like a song.

Words and Music by ADELE ADKINS
and TOBIAS JESSO JR.

To Coda

38

Piano For Two

A VARIETY OF PIANO DUETS FROM HAL LEONARD

THE BEATLES PIANO DUETS – 2ND EDITION

Features 8 arrangements: Can't Buy Me Love • Eleanor Rigby • Hey Jude • Let It Be • Penny Lane • Something • When I'm Sixty-Four • Yesterday.

00290496.. $12.99

GERSHWIN PIANO DUETS

These duet arrangements of 10 Gershwin classics such as "I Got Plenty of Nuttin'," "Summertime," "It Ain't Necessarily So," and "Love Walked In" sound as full and satisfying as the orchestral originals.

00312603.. $12.99

BOB MARLEY FOR PIANO DUET

A unique collection of 10 Marley favorites arranged for piano duet, including: Get Up Stand Up • I Shot the Sheriff • Is This Love • Jamming • No Woman No Cry • One Love • Redemption Song • Stir It Up • and more.

00129926.. $12.99

CONTEMPORARY DISNEY DUETS

8 Disney piano duets to play and perform with a friend! Includes: Almost There • He's a Pirate • I See the Light • Let It Go • Married Life • That's How You Know • Touch the Sky • We Belong Together.

00128259 .... $12.99

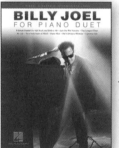

THE SOUND OF MUSIC

9 arrangements from the movie/musical, including: Do-Re-Mi • Edelweiss • Maria • My Favorite Things • So Long, Farewell • The Sound of Music • and more.

00290389.. $12.99

RIVER FLOWS IN YOU AND OTHER SONGS ARRANGED FOR PIANO DUET

10 great songs arranged for 1 piano, 4 hands, including the title song and: All of Me (Piano Guys) • Bella's Lullaby • Beyond • Chariots of Fire • Dawn • Forrest Gump - Main Title (Feather Theme) • Primavera • Somewhere in Time • Watermark.

00141055 .... $12.99

EASY CLASSICAL DUETS

7 great piano duets to perform at a recital, play-for-fun, or sightread! Titles: By the Beautiful Blue Danube (Strauss) • Eine kleine Nachtmusik (Mozart) • Sleeping Beauty Waltz (Tchaikovsky) • and more.

00145767 Book/Online Audio $10.99

BILLY JOEL FOR PIANO DUET

Includes 8 of the Piano Man's greatest hits. Perfect as recital encores, or just for fun! Titles: Just the Way You Are • The Longest Time • My Life • Piano Man • She's Always a Woman • Uptown Girl • and more.

00141139.. $14.99

STAR WARS

8 intergalactic arrangements of *Star Wars* themes for late intermediate to early advanced piano duet, including: Across the Stars • Cantina Band • Duel of the Fates • The Imperial March (Darth Vader's Theme) • Princess Leia's Theme • Star Wars (Main Theme) • The Throne Room (And End Title) • Yoda's Theme.

00119405.. $14.99

Also Available:

HAL LEONARD PIANO DUET PLAY-ALONG SERIES

This great series comes with audio that features separate tracks for the Primo and Secondo parts – perfect for practice and performance! Visit www.halleonard.com for a complete list of titles in the series!

COLDPLAY

Clocks • Paradise • The Scientist • A Sky Full of Stars • Speed of Sound • Trouble • Viva La Vida • Yellow.

00141054.. $14.99

FROZEN

Do You Want to Build a Snowman? • Fixer Upper • For the First Time in Forever • In Summer • Let It Go • Love Is an Open Door • Reindeer(s) Are Better Than People.

00128260.. $14.99

JAZZ STANDARDS

All the Things You Are • Bewitched • Cheek to Cheek • Don't Get Around Much Anymore • Georgia on My Mind • In the Mood • It's Only a Paper Moon • Satin Doll • The Way You Look Tonight.

00290577.. $14.99

TAYLOR SWIFT FOR PIANO DUET

Grab your bestie and start playing 8 Taylor Swift favorites arranged for piano duet! Includes: Blank Space • I Knew You Were Trouble • Love Story • Mine • Shake It Off • Today Was a Fairytale • We Are Never Ever Getting Back Together • You Belong with Me.

00142333.. $12.99

0516